**Bibliographic information published by the German National Library:**

The German National Library lists this publication in the National Bibliography; detailed bibliographic data are available on the Internet at http://dnb.dnb.de .

**Imprint:**

Copyright © 2015 GRIN Verlag, Open Publishing GmbH
Print and binding: Books on Demand GmbH, Norderstedt Germany
ISBN: 978-3-668-03790-8

**This book at GRIN:**

http://www.grin.com/en/e-book/303849/the-future-challenges-of-cybersecurity

Tope Omidiji

# The Future Challenges of CyberSecurity

GRIN Publishing

**GRIN - Your knowledge has value**

Since its foundation in 1998, GRIN has specialized in publishing academic texts by students, college teachers and other academics as e-book and printed book. The website www.grin.com is an ideal platform for presenting term papers, final papers, scientific essays, dissertations and specialist books.

**Visit us on the internet:**

http://www.grin.com/

http://www.facebook.com/grincom

http://www.twitter.com/grin_com

**WEBSTER UNIVERSITY - ITM 5000 07**

# Future Challenges of Cyber Security; Global Attention

**Term Paper**

'Tope Omidiji
7/27/2015

# Introduction

The Internet has brought the world closer than ever, especially, with the ease in sharing information. A post online from Alpine, Texas can be accessible almost immediately by someone in Accra, Ghana and at the same time with the person in Bangalore, India. As much as there is access to the Internet, authorized users can access information/data irrespective of their location. Business activities are now performed globally and efficiently in comfort; buyers and sellers do business without any constraints. Business supporting activities such as paying and receiving of cash, shipping of goods, and other related activities have now been automated in the cyberspace. The most reliable resource vault or knowledge center accessible by all is the Internet; it could even be referred to as one of mankind's greatest achievement. The Internet [Information Technology] revolution became dominant around early 1990's and here are the key areas impacted.

- Trading – Foreign exchange transactions, Forex trading, NASDAQ.
- Marketing – Online Popups, bulk email, and several online marketing dynamics.
- Education – Online degrees, online certification trading, online class registration.
- Entertainment – Music [iTunes, Tidal, YouTube, Spotify], movies and TV shows [Netflix], TV-shows, sports [ESPN online live stream].
- Communication – VOIP, Instant messages, video conferencing and video calls.

- Banking and Transaction – Wire transfers, online transfers, online payment, online banking, EBay, Amazon.

Cyber security assessment

In reality, the Internet or cyberspace as the case maybe has become so attractive, infect, it is now part of our life that we cannot live without. However, it has also made all users including governments, corporate institutions and business entities exposed and vulnerable to numerous cyber crimes. The risk of loosing personal data or theft of an important data like customer data from an organization by cyber criminals has become very high. Cyber security remains the biggest challenge faced by all especially governments and organizations. One of the techniques used in taming cyber crime activities is by tracking and tracing the source of an attack or threat using the IP [Internet Protocol]. The IP and TCP [Transmission Control Protocol] are used to facilitate connection from the source to the destination. They are also classified as source and destination IP's as the case maybe. On a cyber security standpoint, when an IP is successfully tracked, it can help reveal the location of a user [cyber criminal] by displaying the source and destination of the data. Unfortunately, tracking of IP/TCP is no longer effective as they can be changed or manipulated such that it does not reveal their exact location. It is also often used when downloading illegal digital contents like movies. The table below illustrates how a computer network IP-TCP can be hidden/changed, a basic trick commonly used by hackers and users who are about to perform malicious activities online.

3

IP/TCP tracking is still a major form of monitoring online activities; however, one can see that it can be maneuvered and misdirected. A visible IP/TCP from a user may not actually be theirs, especially when they are planning to or already committing some sought of cybercrime.

Individuals, institutions, and governments are faced with the problem of securing their cyberspace, network and information technology infrastructures. Cyber attacks are classified like, from Individuals (online fraudsters and hackers) to other Individuals and institutions attacking other institution to steal data or denial of service. A government can attack another government for political or economic reasons known as state attacks; institutions can do it to one another also. Below examples illustrates recent cyber attacks in different scenarios that made global news headlines.

- Sony Hacking Attack: Incident occurred on 16th of December 2015. Hackers leaked Sony's internal data including that of their employees; the stolen data are categorized as, emails, details of their executive's salaries, and master copies of unreleased movies. The attackers described themselves as GOP [Guardians of Peace]; they stated that their motive is to prevent Sony from releasing the new movie titled "The Interview", which was basically a mockery of North Korean leader "Kim Jong-un". Further investigation on the hacking technique and system used in the attack by the U.S. government showed that it was sponsored by the North Korean Leader allegedly which has also been denied. This even followed a threat by the GOP to lynch terrorist attack on the U.S. soil; however, the movie was released and there was to terror attack till date. Sony's biggest challenge at the time was to stop distribution of hacked materials, they threatened legal actions. Sony succeeded in preventing media organizations and social media platforms like twitter from sharing the hacked material, broadcasting and promoting the incident. According to Los Angeles Time, Sony Corp. has spent an estimated amount of $15 million on post activities from the hacking incident.

- U.S. Federal Workers Cyber Attack: The incident was announced on June 14, 2015. The U.S. agency in charge of records, Office of the Personnel Management (OPM) was hacked. According to Reuters, personal data of about four million U.S. government's current and former federal workers were likely to have been comprised. Law enforcement claimed that all attacks are related to the breach in Anthem and Premera Blue Cross attacks that recently occurred in the U.S (Reuters). It has also been agued by many that the OPM cyber attacks is a means of threatening U.S. foreign policy, national security or economic stability (Reuters). The source of the attack has been alleged to be from China but the Chinese government has maintained innocence and denied all accusations. On July 9, 2015, the OPM confirmed that about 21.5 million people's data have been stolen and comprised from the hacking attack (Reuters). The impact of this incident has not yet been determined as questions regarding the purpose of the attack and what was left behind like malwares in OPM's system are unanswered. This has even led to the resignation of OPM's boss Katherine Archuleta.

- EBay Cyber-Attack: The incident occurred between February and March of 2014 as reported. EBay disclosed that hackers gained access to their internal network thereby might have gained unauthorized access to about 145 million user accounts potentially. The popular e-commerce site reported that there database containing customers' name, telephone numbers, home addresses, date of births, and passwords were hacked. There was major out cry or complaints by customers about the incident because EBay reacted swiftly by asking customers to quickly change their passwords and login details. However, the company's shares still went down 1.73 percent. They also observed reduction in user activity. PayPal, an online payment solution company, which was owned by EBay, was later sold in 2014. This may have been as a result of the attack or a measure to secure their business.

Citing from the three examples from above, one can notice how hard it is to affirm the source of an attack in the cyberspace. Although it can be traced sometimes when properly analyzed by experts; however, the question on weather it is within a particular jurisdiction or not sets in and often times, it is to the detriment of the victim. They focus on determining the impact of such attack and how to implement a more secure system. Governments and Organizations are the most vulnerable to cyber attacks because they have much useful and valuable data targeted by cyber criminals and therefore become a major target for hackers. For Individuals, they are always advised to create more complex password. Investing in cyber security infrastructure is highly recommended to prevent any form of attack by hackers.

Cyberspace is a terminology coined by William Gibson in his book titled Neuromancer (1984). The cyberspace is a domain; technically, it composed electronics/electromagnetism where data is transferred, stored, and utilized through devices (computers, smart phones etc.) when connected to a network system. This is a domain where billions of users from across the world can share experience on daily basis. In fact, it has been described as a place where humans from all over the world are able to interact and connect with one another through computers and telecommunication. The cyberspace is a virtual world where everyone seeks richness and complexity. It is not just about the Internet but a community where everything is possible and nothing is impossible. Although cyberspace has brought about a lot of possibility and ease of life to our world; however, this ideology has also enabled crimes; mostly, financial related as illustrated in the following examples.

- Money Laundering: An easy access to facilities that aids activity through the cyber space. Paying advisors to help them set up corporations with anonymous ownership. The mechanism used is International Business Corporations and Offshore Financial Centers. Corrupt government officials are able to move huge some of money offshore to where they feel its safe and untraceable.

- Fraud: Scammers are now able to use anonymous credit cards, bank accounts, concealed global telephone numbers [customized location], and false passports, which can all be purchased online. They are considered as tools used by scammers in defrauding their victims. Hackers mostly provide them and sell within their community.

- Identity Theft: Hackers can now use information aggregation or aggregate information to steal people's identity for their malicious use. Cyber criminals have taken advantage of the fact that they can have access to other people's information without them knowing about it and then use it for their criminal activities.

The concept of cyber space is to implement what is not physically visible but available in the virtual world into reality or visibility; unfortunately, people with malicious and fraudulent intentions online often misrepresent this.

Corporations and individuals need to take precautionary steps to protect any type of hacking [amateur or professional], they also need to understand what their top vulnerability is. For example, home LANs (Local Area Network) and Wi-Fi are the least secured and vulnerable to amateur hacking. Amateur hacking often lead to crimes like illegal use of existing credit cards, use of accounts (checking or savings), and use of generated personal information for criminal activities. Criminals to obtain loans, open new accounts, and use of passport and ID cards to commit crime mostly use these types of generated or stolen personal information.

For example, there are precautionary measures users can take to protect their personal information, as well as corporations. The least LAN/Wi-Fi home users can do to protect themselves against amateur hacking is to be aware of email dirty tricks and authorization passwords. They must be sure not to open any strange link received in an email or in their browser. Information concerning access to LAN/Wi-Fi such as pin codes, passwords and account information must not be shared or displayed publicly. For safety purpose, it is recommended that passwords should be created alphanumerically and must be difficult to guess.

According to the National Crime Victimization Survey (NCVS), identity theft can be categorized into three major aspects or scenarios as the case may be. They are referred to as "unauthorized use or attempted use of an existing account, personal information to open any new account, and any misuse of personal information with a motive to use them for fraudulent purpose (Bureau of Justice Statistics)." It has been observed that a little more than half of the victims of identity theft who succeeded in resolving identity theft related problems all occurred within the same day (Harrell and

Langton).  However, the most reported form of identity theft is the illegal use of existing account holder information. This is considered as fraud, a situation where stolen credit cards or bank account details are used for unauthorized transactions by a third party. Over 85% of reported identity theft cases were credit card and bank account fraud (Harrell and Langton). Identity theft is considered to be very critical as the impact cannot be controlled or limited to a particular locality.

In 2013, the Consumer Sentinel Network (CSN) Data Book recorded two million consumer complaints and 14% were relating from identity theft. This information was gathered by CSN from various federal government agencies. There were 280,000 identity theft complaints in 2013 according to CSN; the table below shows a statistics of identity theft related crimes.

| Categories of Identity Theft Complaints Reported in 2013 | Percentage of 280,000 Identity Theft Cases Reported |
|---|---|
| Government documents/benefits fraud | 34% |
| Credit card fraud | 17% |
| Telephone and utilities fraud | 14% |
| Bank fraud | 8% |
| Employment related fraud | 6% |
| Loan fraud | 4% |

Source: https://www.ftc.gov/system/files/.../reports/...2013/sentinel-cy2013.pdf, page 3

Companies are required to keep customer information as safe as possible in order not to lose credibility which may lead to decline in revenue. Information security incidence has been on the rise up to over 50% and both small and large businesses have been ensuring to keep their business and customers protected. Consequently, IT budget on security is still reported low. It has appeared that less attention has been paid to cyber security, this is reflected in most organizations IT budget. Taking cybercrimes more seriously should be an action that should be taken with all seriousness and urgency. According to PwC, there has been a 48% increase in number of cybersecurity reported incident in 2014. They conducted a research among company executives in about 160 countries. The table below illustrates and compares IT spending and IT security spending.

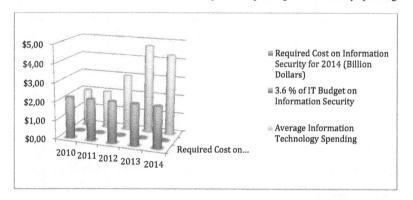

Online Scamming

This section described online scamming from Nigeria as a case study. It started at the time when businesses began to establish cyber cafes in Nigeria around the year 2000. Lagos, Nigeria was the biggest platform, one of the most populated cities in the world. However, nothing could be done online locally and effectively until about five years later. Schools, banks, government, churches, services had nothing to offer on the Internet. Internet browsing in Nigeria at that time was considered by young people [customer patronizing cyber café's] as just an adventure, a way to see what was going on in the other part of world. Youths were exited to start "browsing" just because Internet was

11

new, different, and fun. It was the new way to be identified. They even get dates at these cybercafé's, teach their girlfriends or date how to browse the Internet. In some cases, they get paid to teach others how to use the Internet or open an email for others. The ability to use the Internet and not just the computer became a skill that could make some income. Suddenly, people started joining dating sites and online chat room like yahoo, the most popular and free chartroom around that time. Online dating became popular suddenly, mostly with the hope that their partners they will come get them out of their miserable Nigeria or perhaps send some money. Quite a few people travelled out of the country to meet their partner, some got gifts and money occasionally and on their special days. The youth's especially young boy started putting up fake stories, lies, and different mechanism to extort money from their online dates. A young boy could pose as a pretty young lady to attack rich men or keep their bio and seek for rich older women. This was the birth of the famous Yahoo boys; they were getting money in all different kind of ways. Today, the term "yahoo boy" has moved to not just dating to different kind of fraudulent activities online.

Even though no one should be blamed for this; not even the owners of those cyber cafe's, this was simple a case of having what was not needed locally, the government had no mechanism to make the internet relevant as at then or even monitor activities. "Yahoo yahoo" became so popular; it even saved a lot of people from extreme poverty. Not and never in support of this fraudulent activities but sometimes, one will wonder what would have become of the so many unemployed poor young boys if there were no "yahoo yahoo". Things has become so bad that Nigerians are now known worldwide for internet fraud, the most popular form of Internet scamming from Nigeria is the dating and 419

12

(advance fee fraud) all based on manipulation. This is because there is an inefficient local monitoring and difficult for countries who's citizens are victims to act without corporation of the local authority. The stories/lies related to these activities are listed in points below.

- I am in the Military on a foreign mission
- My father left me treasury
- Fake business proposal
- Fake check and fake bank account deposit

The 419 scam has existed long before the existence of Internet in Nigeria, the Internet only became a means to deliver the "product faster" through the cyberspace. A single or perhaps lonely 60 year old rich woman will be convinced with sweet words to believe that she has found love again, and off course a much younger lover in there 20's. Also, they make people believe that an unknown relative had left a huge some of money that no one ever knew about. The reality is both the criminal and victim are always interested in something they cannot find easily. It is like a contest or game; in a game we always have a winner and a looser. Most governments like The U.S. have been making a lot of effort to reduce these activities through awareness campaign and cyber monitoring. Users are meant to take stories with a pinch of salt when dealing online; checking for reviews can be helpful. Validating every information is very important, we all have to be very conscious online.

The cyber community is a global community; unfortunately, while some governments put adequate laws in place, other governments may not. Hackers and malicious individuals prefer to live and attack in countries where laws are not enforced or the authorities are corrupt. Here are some discoveries according to the 2015 Internet Security Threat Report, Volume 20 base on Symantec Global Intelligence Network.

- Understanding how cyber attackers are able to successfully plunge in an organizations cooperate defense, which is also be referred to as their demilitarized zone [DMZ]. Also, considering the fact that cybercriminals are hedging over cooperate organization in terms of defense is quite alarming. Organizations need to be more proactive in terms of implementing measures and putting accurate systems in place to protect IT infrastructure. Cyber hackers are searching and learning on how to break into multiple systems as much as they can for their criminal purposes. They are continuously researching for ways to break into systems no matter how complex it is.

- The rise in ransomeware attacks escalated over a 100% in the year 2014. Online users are growing daily, the opportunity is endless and the risk is getting much higher.

- The use of social media networks and mobile apps to facilitate attacks by cybercriminals. For example, it takes nothing to set up a fake twitter account of a known person to perform malicious activity. Verification of accounts has been used to reduce attack and damage on public figures unless their verified account is hacked.

- Taking cybercrimes more serious than ever. Limiting cyber security attacks is everyone's responsibility. We all have to be conscious and not relenting on putting in place stringent measures online.

All Internet users should carry out the responsibility of securing the cyberspace religiously, global cyber security awareness. In the coming years as the cyberspace begin to grow; our dependency on the Internet will also expand. Internet users have tripled within the last ten years, over One billion users in 2005 to over three billion Internet users in 2015 according to statista. Almost half of the world's population is active Internet users and with the current trend, there is a possibility of having at least six billion Internet users in 2025. This will require more stringent and precautionary measures; new laws on cyberspace/Internet will be required and more complex systems will be required as the world gradually emerge into a cyber world. This will enable accountability and reliability on the Internet. Below are the expected changes.

Proposal; Global Attention

- Internet User Login: As part of measures to track Internet activities, all users may be required to have logins. Username and password or unique Internet code to gain access. This will help identify each user online.

- Global Cyber Law: There should be accepted global laws governing cyber activities to limit and prevent cyber attacks. This will address the issues related to jurisdiction, the laws will be applicable to all Internet users regardless of their locations.

- Cyber Security Firm: The requirement to develop and implement systems to prevent and limit cyber attacks will increase. Consequently, there will be a major growth in terms of revenue and size of cyber security firms. There will be more proactivity in implementing cyber security systems, performing quality and security checks, and more amounts will be allocated to IT security budget. This is now a time to invest in cyber security stocks.

Cyber crime will increase, awareness will also increase, and cyber security companies will acquire more financial gains. However, in other to achieve a secured cyberspace, there will have to be a global monitoring organization that would not be limited by jurisdiction with the ability to monitor, enforce, regulate and prosecute. With the recent sporadic cyber attacks on major institutions and organizations especially in the U.S, this matter will have to be addressed as soon as possible.

## Works Cited

Lynch, James P. "Bureau of Justice Statistics (BJS) - Identity Theft." *Bureau of Justice Statistics (BJS) - Identity Theft.* Bureau of Justice Statistics, 06 Nov. 2014. Web. 07 Nov. 2014. http://www.bjs.gov/index.cfm?ty=tp&tid=42

Momin, Nakib. "Subscribe To Get FREE Tutorials!" *Change Your Ip in Less Then 1 Minute.* IP ADDRESS, WINDOWS, 11 Nov. 2011. Web. 02 July 2015.

Mickelberg, Kevin, Neal Pollard, and Laurie Schive. *US Cybercrime : Rising Risks, Reduced Readiness: Key Findings from the 2014 US State of Cybercrime Survey.* United States: PricewaterhouseCoopers, 2014. *www.pwc.com/cybersecurity.* Web. 6 Dec. 2014.

"Number of Worldwide Internet Users from 2000 to 2015 (in Millions)." *Statista.* The Statistics Portal, n.d. Web. 19 July 2015. http://www.statista.com/statistics/273018/number-of-internet-users-worldwide/

Rouse, Margaret, and Effrey Cox. "Cyberspace Definition." *Searchsoa.techtarget.com.* SOA Jeff, 08 May 2013. Web. 07 June 2015.

SPETALNICK, MATT, and DAVID BRUNNSTROM. "China in Focus as Cyber Attack Hits Millions of U.S. Federal Workers." *Reuters|Technology.* Reuters, 5 June 2015. Web. 07 July 2015. http://searchsoa.techtarget.com/definition/cyberspace

"2015 Internet Security Threat Report, Volume 20." *Symantec Corporation Highlights from the 2015.* Internet Security Threat Report, n.d. Web. 09 July 2015. https://www4.symantec.com/mktginfo/whitepaper/ISTR/21347931_GA-internet-security-threat-report-volume-20-2015-appendices.pdf

The Internet has brought the world closer than ever, especially, with the ease in sharing information. A post online from Alpine, Texas can be accessible almost immediately by someone in Accra, Ghana and at the same time with the person in Bangalore, India. As much as there is access to the Internet, authorized users can access information/data irrespective of their location. (...)

www.grin.com

Document Nr. V303849
http://www.grin.com
ISBN 978-3-668-03790-8